PROBLEM SOLVING™

WITH MATH MODELS

FOURTH GRADE

DR. NICKI NEWTON

Gigglenook Publication
P.O. Box 110134
Trumbull CT 06611
Email: gigglenook@gmail.com
Website: www.drnicki123.com

Produced by GiggleNook Publications
Thank you to the entire Production staff

Chief Operating Officer: Dr. Nicki Newton
Publisher: Gigglenook Publication
Cover Design: This Way Up Productions

Printed in the United States of America through CreateSpace, LLC
ISBN-13: 978-1493521944
ISBN-10: 1493521942
Volume 1: December 2012

Dedicated to Mom and Pops, Always

PROBLEM SOLVING™

With Math Models

Fourth Grade

Dr. Nicki Newton

TABLE OF CONTENTS

FOREWORD

Story problems can be great! Story problems are the stuff life is made of. If we can make connections for children between their daily lives and the problems we pose and solve in school, we will have much more success. We need to provide scaffolds into the process.

The New Math Common Core (2010) places a big emphasis on problem solving. The first mathematical practice mentioned states that students should "Make sense of problems and persevere in solving them." It goes on to describe this by stating that mathematically proficient students should be able to explain a problem and find ways to enter into it. According to the New Math Common Core students should be able to solve problems with objects, drawings and equations. In this book, students will practice word problems aligned to the standards by using the CCSS designated math models.

The Math Common Core, actually adopted the framework for story problems, created by Carpenter, Fennema, Franke, Levi & Empson, 1999; Peterson, Fennema & Carpenter (1989). The research says that the more teachers understand these types of problems and teach them to their students, the better students understand the problems and are able to solve them. Furthermore, the research makes the case that the KEY WORD METHOD should be avoided! Students should learn to understand the problem types and what they are actually discussing rather than "key word" tricks. The thing about key words is that they only work with really simplistic problems and so as students do more sophisticated work with word problems, the key words do not serve them well. They may actually lead them in the wrong direction, often encouraging the wrong operation. For example, given this problem: *John has 2 apples. Kate has 3 more than he does. How many do they have altogether?* Many students just add 2 and 3 instead of unpacking the problem. Another example, given this problem: *Sue has 10 marbles. She has 2 times as many marbles as Lucy. How many marbles does Lucy have?*

Often times, students just multiply because they see the word times, instead of really reading and understanding the problem.

This book is about giving students a repertoire of tools, models and strategies to help them think about, understand and solve word problems. We want to scaffold reasoning opportunities from the concrete (using objects) to the pictorial (pictures and drawings) and, finally, to the abstract (writing equations).

DR. NICKI NEWTON

ACKNOWLEDGEMENTS

I would like to thank many people for their support, expertise, guidance, and encouragement during this project. First of all I would like to thank God, without him this would not be possible. Second, I would like to thank my mom, pa, big mom, and granddaddy. Third, I would like to thank my family for all their love and support, especially my Tia that calls me every day and asks me "What have you accomplished today?" And I would like to thank all of my friends that support me all the time. Finally, I would like to thank the many people who were part of the Gigglenook Book Production Team. This book series would not have been possible without the continual support of all of them.

Introduction to the Types of Word Problems

Grade Specific Problem Solving Expectations

The CCSSM (2010) is very specific about what students should be able to do in terms of solving word problems by grade level. There are 4 general categories for addition and subtraction problems. In kindergarten students are exposed to 4 problem types - 1 addition, 1 subtraction, and 2 part/part whole problems. They are expected to work with these types of problems through 10. But, in first grade, there is a big leap. The standards say that the children will be able to work with the above-mentioned four problems, in addition to addition and subtraction change unknown problems, the other part/ part whole problem as well as comparison problems with unknowns in all positions and with a symbol for the unknown to represent the problem through 20. They should also be able to solve word problems with three numbers adding up to 20. By second grade, they have to do the same thing with all problem types, including the harder comparison problems through 100. In 3rd through 5th grade the students should be able to solve all of the problem types using larger whole numbers, fractions and decimals.

Adding to Problems

"Adding to" problems are all about adding. There are three types. The first type is *Adding to* problems where the result is unknown. For example, *Jenny had 5 marbles. John gave her 3 more. How many marbles does Jenny have now?* In this problem the result is unknown. Teachers tend to tell these types of problems. They are basic and straightforward. The teacher should start with concrete items, then proceed to drawing out the story, then to diagramming the story, and finally to using equations to represent the story. This is the easiest type of story problem to solve.

The second kind of *Adding to* problem is the "Change Unknown" problem. For example, *Jenny had 5 marbles. John gave her some more. Now she has 8 marbles. How many marbles did John give her?* In this type of problem, the students are looking for the change. They know the start and they know the end but they don't know the *change*. So, students have to put down the start and then count up to find how many. Students could also start with 8 marbles and take away the original 5 to see how many more were added to make 8.

The third type of *Adding to* Problem is a "Start Unknown" problem. For example, *Jenny had some marbles. John gave her 3 more. Now she has 8 marbles. How many marbles did Jenny have in the beginning?* In this type of problem, the students are looking for the start. This is the hardest type of *adding to* problem to solve. This takes a great deal of modeling.

Taking From Problems

Taking From problems are all about subtracting. There are three types. The first type is *taking fro*m problems where the result is unknown. For example, *Jenny had 5 marbles. She gave John 3. How many marbles does Jenny have left?* In this problem, the result is unknown. Teachers tend to tell these types of problems. They are basic and straightforward. The teacher should start with concrete items, then proceed to drawing out the story, then to diagramming the story, and finally to writing equations to represent the story.

The second kind of *Taking From* problem is the "Change Unknown" problem. For example, *Jenny had 10 marbles. She gave John some. Now she has 8 marbles left. How many marbles did she give to John?* In this type of problem, the students are looking for the change. They know the start and they know the end but they don't know the *change*. So, students have to put down the start and then count up to find how many. Students could also start with 10 marbles and take away some until they have 8 left. They would count to see how many they had to take away to remain with 8.

The third type of *Taking From* problem is a "Start Unknown" problem. For example, *Jenny had some marbles. She gave John 3. Now she has 7 marbles left. How many marbles did Jenny have to start with?* In this type of problem, the students are looking for the start. This is the hardest type of *taking from* problem to solve. This takes a great deal of modeling. You can use ten frames to show this. One strategy is to have the students put down the seven she has left and count up three to see how many that makes.

Part/Part Whole Problems

A *Part/Part Whole* problem is a problem that discusses the two parts and the whole. There are three types of *Part/Part Whole* Problems. The first is a problem where the *whole* is unknown. For example, *Susie has some marbles. Five are red and five are blue. How many marbles does she have altogether?* We know both parts and the task is to figure out the whole.

The second kind of problem is a problem where one of the *parts* is unknown. For example, *Susie has 10 marbles. Seven are red. The rest are blue. How many are blue?* In this type of problem, we are given the whole and one of the parts. The task is to figure out the other part.

The third type of problem is a *Both Addends Unknown* problem. In this type of problem both addends are not known, only the total is given. For example, *There are 4 frogs on the log. Some are blue and some are green. There are some of each color. How many of each color could there be?* The task is to figure out all the possible combinations.

Comparing Stories

Comparing Stories are the most difficult types of stories to tell. There are three types of comparison stories. The first type of comparing story is where two different things are being compared. For example, *Susie has ten lollipops and Kayla had eight. How many more lollipops did Susie have than Kayla?*

The second type of comparing story is where the bigger part is unknown. In this type of story, we are looking for the bigger amount. For example, *Susie had 4 candies. Maya had 3 more than her. How many candies did Maya have?* Here, we know what Susie had, and then in comparison, Maya had 3 more. The task is to find the bigger part.

The third type of comparing story is to find the smaller part. This is the hardest type of story to tell. For example, *Jaya has 7 candies. She has 3 more than Marcos. How many does Marcos have? In this type of story we know what Jaya has and we know that she has 3 more than Marcos.* We are looking for the smaller amount. We only know about what Marcos has in comparison to what Jaya has. The task is to use the information given to solve for the smaller part.

Two Step Problems

Starting in second grade, students start to do two-step problems where they combine the problem types. For example: *Sue had 5 more marbles than David. David had 4 marbles. How many marbles do they have altogether?* To solve two-step problems, students should have a good understanding of the original problem types and then these are combined into a more complex problem.

The 4th Grade Word Problem Standards (CCSSM, 2010)

4OA3: Solve multistep word problems posed with whole numbers. Represent these problems using equations with a letter standing for the unknown quantity.

4NF3: Solve word problems involving addition and subtraction, e.g., by using visual fraction models and equations to represent the problem.

4NF7: Compare two decimals to hundredths…Record the results of comparisons with the symbols >, =, or <, and justify the conclusions, e.g., by using a visual model.

4MD1: Know relative sizes of measurement units within one system of units including km, m, cm; kg, g; lb., oz.; l, ml; hr, min, sec. Record measurement equivalents in a two-column table.

4MD2: Use the four operations to solve word problems involving distances, intervals of time, liquid volumes, masses of objects, and money, including problems involving simple fractions or decimals, and problems that require expressing measurements given in a larger unit in terms of a smaller unit.

4MD3: Apply the area and perimeter formulas for rectangles in real world and mathematical problems.

4MD4: Make a line plot to display a data set of measurements in fractions of a unit (1/2, 1/4, 1/8). Solve problems involving addition and subtraction of fractions by using information presented in line plots.

4MD7: Solve addition and subtraction problems to find unknown angles on a diagram in real world and mathematical problems, e.g., by using an equation with a symbol for the unknown angle measure.

INTRODUCING THE MODELS FOR THINKING

There are several great tools to use for solving number stories. In this book students will use a few different tools to think about the word problems. The CCSSM (2010) Standards state that students should use "objects, drawings, diagrams and acting out" to solve problems. In 4th grade students should be able to:

USE EQUATIONS

4OA3: Represent problems using equations with a letter standing for the unknown quantity.

$$4 + x = 29$$

$$345 - x = 49$$

4MD7: Recognize angle measure as additive. Use an equation with a symbol for the unknown angle measure to solve problems.

$$56^\circ + 34^\circ + x = 180^\circ$$

USE DRAWINGS

4NF3: Use visual fraction models and equations to represent the problem.

4NF7: Compare decimals with the symbols >, =, or <, and justify the conclusions, e.g., by using a visual model.

$.40 > .25$ $.8 < .9$ $.50 + .20 = .70$

USE TABLES

4MD1: Record measurement equivalents in a two-column table.

Centimeters	Meters
100	1
200	2
300	3
400	4
500	5

USE OPEN NUMBERLINES

4MD2: Represent measurement quantities using diagrams such as number line diagrams that feature a measurement scale.

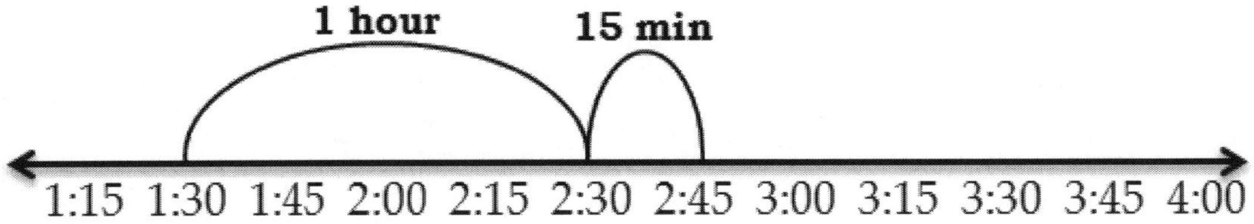

Students also use the open number line for other types of problems. They draw a line, plot numbers on it and count using a variety of strategies. For example, let's take the problem 45 plus 37.

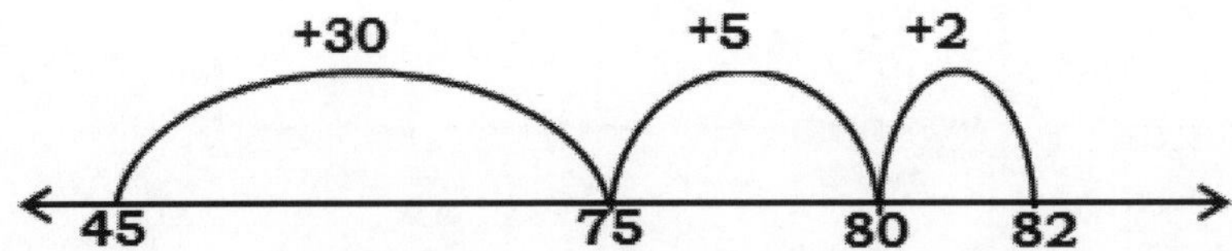

The student starts at 45 and jumps 30 because they broke apart the 37 into 30, plus 5, plus 2. From 75, they jump five more to 80 and then 2 more to 82. Number lines are a huge part of the new math CCSS and it is very important to make sure that students are very comfortable using them. Students will use number lines throughout the different grades.

USE DOUBLE OPEN NUMBER LINE

The double number line is a great model for comparing two different things. For example, *Sue had 15 apples and Josie had 4 more than she did. How many did Josie have?*

Students draw a line and then plot one part of the comparison on the top and the other part of the comparison on the bottom. (See below)

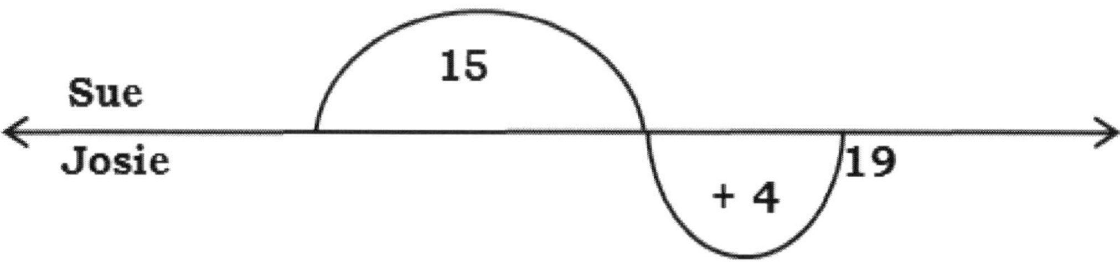

USE FORMULAS

4MD3: Apply the area and perimeter formulas for rectangles in real world and mathematical problems.

Perimeter = 2(length + width)

Area = L x W

CREATE LINE PLOTS

4MD4: Make a line plot to display a data set of measurements in fractions of a unit (1/2, 1/4, 1/8). Solve problems involving addition and subtraction of fractions by using information presented in line plots.

The 4th grade made a frequency table of sizes of plants. Use the data in the frequency table to make a line plot.

4½, 5, 5, 5, 5, 6, 7, 7, 7, 7, 7, 7½, 7½, 7½

Line plot of pets per person in our classroom

							x	
					x		x	
					x		x	x
					x		x	x
				x	x	x	x	x
1	2	3	4	4½	5	6	7	7½

Line plot questions:

1. What was the length of the longest flower?
2. What was the length of the shortest flower?
3. What is the difference between the lengths of the shortest and longest flowers?

USE BAR/TAPE DIAGRAM

In the CCSSM students are required to know how to use a tape diagram to model their thinking. *Bar diagrams help students to "unpack" the structure of a problem and lay the foundation for its solution" (Diezmann and English, 2001, p. 77 cited in Charles, Monograph 24324). Nickerson (1994) found that the ability to use diagrams is integral to mathematics thinking and learning (cited in Charles).*

In the charts below, I have provided a detailed explanation for each of the CCSS 1-step word problem types for addition and subtraction. The word problem type is designated with a sample problem. Then there is a bar diagram to show the relationships between the quantities. Then there is an explanation of the problem type and the various strategies that can be used to solve the problem. There is also the algebraic equation showing the different operations that can be used to solve the problem. As Charles (Monograph 24324) points out, *"It is important to recognize that a relationship in some word problems can be translated into more than one appropriate number sentence."*

Problem Types	Result Unknown	Change Unknown	Start Unknown
Join/Adding to	Marco had 5 marbles. His brother gave him 5 more. How many does he have now?	Marco had 5 marbles. His brother gave him some more. Now he has 10. How many did his brother give him?	Marco had some marbles. His brother gave him 5 more. Now he has 10. How many did he have in the beginning?
Bar Diagram Modeling Problem	? ⟷ [5 | 5]	10 ⟷ [5 | ?]	10 ⟷ [? | 5]
What are we looking for? Where is X?	Both addends are known. We are looking for the total amount. The result is the unknown. In other words, we know what we started with and we know the change, we are looking for the end.	The first addend is known. The result is also known. We are looking for the change. The change is unknown. In other words, we know what happened at the start and we know what happened at the end. We are looking for the change. We need to find out what happened in the middle.	The second addend is known. The result is known. We are looking for the start. The start is unknown. In other words, we know the change and we know the end but we don't know what happened at the beginning.
Algebraic Sentence	5 + 5 = ?	5 + ?= 10 10-5=?	x + 5 = 10
Strategies to Solve	Add/ Know number Bonds/Know derived Facts/ Count Up	Count Up/Know Bonds/	Count up/Subtract
Answer	5 + 5 = 10 He had ten marbles.	5 + 5 = 10 10 - 5 = 5 He brother gave him five marbles.	5 + 5 = 10 10 - 5 = 5 He had five marbles.

Problem Types	Result Unknown	Change Unknown	Start Unknown
Separate/ Taking From	Marco had 10 marbles. He gave his brother 4. How many does he have left?	Marco had 10 marbles. He gave some away. Now he has 5 left. How many did he give away?	Marco had some marbles. He gave 2 away and now he has 5 left. How many did he have to start with?
Bar Diagram Modeling Problem	10 4 | ?	10 ? | 5	1? 5 | 5
What are we looking for? Where is X?	In this story we know the beginning and what happened in the middle. The mystery is what happened at the end. The result is unknown.	In this story we know the beginning and the end. The mystery is what happened in the middle. The change is unknown.	In this story we know what happened in the middle and what happened at the end. The mystery is how did it start. The start is unknown.
Algebraic Sentence	10 - 4 =?	10 – ? = 5 5 + x =10	? - 2 = 5 2 + 5 =?
Strategies to Solve	Subtract/ /Use number Bonds Facts/ Know derived Facts (Doubles -1, Doubles -2)	Subtract until you have the result left/ Count Up/Use number Bonds/Use derived facts	Count up/Subtract
Answer	10-4 = 6 He had 6 marbles left.	10-5=5 5 + 5 = 10 He gave away 5 marbles.	7-2=5 2+5=7 He had 7 marbles in the beginning.

Problem Types	Quantity Unknown	Part Unknown	Both Addends Unknown
Part/Part Whole/Putting together/Taking Apart	Marco has 5 red marbles and 5 blue ones. How many marbles does Marco have? 5 + 5 = x	Marco has 10 marbles. Five are red and the rest are blue. How many are blue? 10 -5 = or 5 + x = 10	Marco has 10 marbles. Some are red and some are blue. How many could be red and how many could be blue?
Bar Diagram Modeling Problem	? 5 | 5	10 5 | ?	10 ? | ?
What are we looking for? Where is X?	In this type of story we are talking about a group, set or collection of something. Here we know both parts and we are looking for the total.	In this type of story we are talking about a group, set or collection of something. Here we know the total and one of the parts. We are looking for the amount of the other part.	In this type of story we are talking about a group, set or collection of something. Here we know the total but we are to think about all the possible ways to make the group, set or collection.
Algebraic Sentence	5 + 5 = ?	5 + ? = 10 10-5=?	x + y = 10
Strategies to Solve	Add/ Know number Bonds/Know derived Facts/ Count Up	Count Up/Know Bonds/	Count up/Subtract
Answer	5+5=10 He had ten marbles.	5+5=10 10-5 =? Five were blue	1+9 4+6 9+1 6+4 2+8 5+5 8 + 2 3+7 10+0 0 +10 7+3 These are the possibilities

Problem Types	Difference Unknown	Bigger Part Unknown	Smaller Part Unknown
Compare	Marco has 5 marbles. His brother has 7. How many more marbles does his brother have than he does?	Marco has 5 marbles. His brother has 2 more than he does. How many marbles does his brother have?	Tom has 5 rocks. Marco has 2 less than Tom. How many rocks does Marco have?
Bar Diagram Modeling Problem	[5] ? ⟷ [7]	[5] [5][2] ?	[5] [?]
What are we looking for? Where is X?	In this type of story we are comparing two amounts. We are looking for the difference between the two numbers.	In this type of story we are comparing two amounts. We are looking for the bigger part which is unknown.	In this type of story we are comparing two amounts. We are looking for the smaller part which is unknown.
Algebraic Sentence	7-5 =?	5 + ? = 7	5-2=?
Strategies to Solve	Count up/ Count back	Count up	Subtract
Answer	His brother had 2 more marbles than he did.	His brother had 7 marbles.	Marco had 3 marbles.

TEACHER TIPS:

- When you introduce the problem, be sure to tell the students what type of problem it is.
- Remember that you can take the same problem and rework it in different ways throughout the week.
- Work on a problem type until the students are proficient at recognizing and solving that problem type. Also give them opportunities to write and tell that specific problem type.
- Be sure to contextualize the problems in the students' everyday lives. Using the problems in the book as models, substitute the students' names and their everyday things.
- Be sure to provide tons of guided practice. Solve problems together as a class, with partners and in groups. Individual practice should come after the students have had plenty of opportunities to work together and comprehend and understand what they are doing.
- Emphasize that there is no one correct way to solve a problem but that there is usually only one correct answer.
- Encourage students to always show their work

CHAPTER 1
ADD TO RESULT UNKNOWN PROBLEMS

These types of problems are the easiest types of addition problems. In these problems students are looking for what happened at the end of the story. We know what we started with and what we added to that part. We are trying to find out how many we have altogether now.

PROBLEM	John had 10 marbles. Henry gave him 7 more. How many does he have now?
MODEL	+7 10 17
EQUATION	10 + 7 = ?

Add to Result Unknown

1. Song A had 17,999 downloads on Monday. On Tuesday, it had 34,845 more downloads. How many downloads did it have altogether?

Way#1: Use friendly numbers to add. Which place could you round to get a friendly number in order to add quickly?

Way#2: Write an equation with a letter standing for the unknown.

Explain your thinking:

ADD TO RESULT UNKNOWN

2. Brett left his house at 7:05 a.m. He spent 45 minutes at Kurt's house and 25 minutes at Tom's house. How long was Brett gone?

Solve with an open number line

Explain your thinking:

ADD TO RESULT UNKNOWN

3. Lauren, the baker, used 557 grams of sugar in the cake mixture. Then she used 528 grams of sugar for the frosting. How many grams of sugar did she use for the cake altogether? Did she use more than a kilogram of sugar to make the cake?

Model with a tape diagram

Explain your thinking:

ADD TO RESULT UNKNOWN

4. Andy made fruit punch. First, he added 134 ml of cranberry juice, then he added 358 ml of pineapple juice, finally, he added 442 ml of banana juice. How many ml of juice did Andy put into the fruit punch altogether? Did he use more than a liter?

Model with a tape diagram

Explain your thinking:

Add to Result Unknown

5. Jake had $99.10. He got $55.20 for his birthday. How much money does he have now?

Way#1: Solve with an equation

Way#2: Check in a different way

Explain your thinking:

ADD TO RESULT UNKNOWN

6. Miguel ran 2/3 of a mile in the morning and 1/3 of a mile in the afternoon. Did Miguel run over a mile?

Way#1: Solve with a number line

Way#2: Solve with a drawing

Explain your thinking:

ADD TO RESULT UNKNOWN

7. Farmer Kate built a yard for her chickens to run around in. It was 7 ft. long and 7 ft. wide. She found it to be too short. So she added 9 more feet to the length. What was the length of the fence with the addition? What was the perimeter of the fence with the addition? What is the area of the fence with the addition?

Draw an illustration to solve

Explain your thinking:

Add to Result Unknown

8. Brittany made necklaces. She had 3ft. of string. She could make 1 necklace with 12 inches of string. How many necklaces can she make with 3 ft. of string?

Create a table to show your thinking

Necklace	Inches	Feet
1	12	1

Explain your thinking:

Chapter 1 Quiz: Add to Result Unknown

Solve with a model:

1. Fran made some fruit punch. She put in a quart of orange juice. Then she added a quart of apple juice. Finally, she added a quart of pineapple juice. How much fruit punch did she make? Did she make a gallon of punch? Show your work.

2. Clay made a dog run in his backyard. At first, he made a run that was 5ft. long and 5ft. wide. Then he decided to make it bigger. He added 2ft. to the length and 3ft. to the width. What is the perimeter of the new dog run? What is the area of the new dog run?

3. Maria ran 555 meters in the morning and 488 meters in the afternoon. How many meters did she run altogether? Did she run more than a kilometer?

4. Kelly had 3/6 of a yard of blue string. She bought 2/6 of a yard of yellow string and 4/6 of a yard of orange string. How much string does she have now? Does she have more than a yard?

CHAPTER 2
ADD TO CHANGE UNKNOWN PROBLEMS

In these problems students are looking for what happened in the middle of the story. In this type of story we know what happened at the beginning but then some change happened and now we have more than we started with at the end. We are trying to find out how many things were added in the middle of the story.

PROBLEM	John had 5 marbles. His mother gave him some more. Now he has 12. How many did his mother give him?
MODEL	+7 5 12
EQUATION	5 + ? = 12

ADD TO CHANGE UNKNOWN

1. The candy store had 435 grams of chocolate fudge. They made some more fudge and now they have1000 grams. How many grams of chocolate did they make?

Way#1: Solve with a number line

Way#2: Solve with an equation, use a letter for the unknown

Explain your thinking:

ADD TO CHANGE UNKNOWN

2. Javier went to the basketball court at 2:15 p.m. He went home at 4:07 p.m. How long was he at the basketball court?

Solve with a number line diagram

Explain your thinking:

ADD TO CHANGE UNKNOWN

3. Mr. Leroy walked 3/6 of a mile in the morning. In the afternoon he walked some more. By the end of the day he had walked 1 mile. How much did he walk in the afternoon?

Way#1: Solve with a number line

Way#2: Solve with an illustration

Explain your thinking:

ADD TO CHANGE UNKNOWN

4. Dina made fruit punch for the party. She added 400 ml of cherry juice and then some apple juice. Altogether, she had 1 liter of juice. How much apple juice did she use?

Way#1: Draw a picture of a beaker to solve

Way#2: Solve with an equation, use a letter for the unknown

Explain your thinking:

ADD TO CHANGE UNKNOWN

5. Sharon had $33.54. She got some more money for her birthday. Now she has $50.59. How much money did she get for her birthday?

Way#1: Solve with an equation, use a letter for the unknown

Way#2: Solve another way

Explain your thinking:

ADD TO CHANGE UNKNOWN

6. In a jumping competition, Kara jumped 55 centimeters for her first jump and then some more centimeters for her second jump. Altogether, she jumped 100 centimeters. How much did she jump for her second jump?

Way#1: Solve with an open number line

Way#2: Solve with an equation, use a letter for the unknown

Explain your thinking:

ADD TO CHANGE UNKNOWN

7. Farmer Sue built a fence for her rabbits. First she made a fence that was 7ft long and 7 ft. wide. Then she added some length to the fence. Now the length is 10 ft. long. How many feet did she add to the length of the fence altogether? What is the new perimeter of the yard?

Way#1: Solve with drawing

Way#2: Solve with an equation, use a letter for the unknown

Explain your thinking:

ADD TO CHANGE UNKNOWN

8. The bakery only had 3 ounces of fudge left in the morning. It made some more and now it has a pound. How many ounces of fudge did the bakery make?

Way#1: Model with a tape diagram

Way#2: Solve with an equation, use a letter for the unknown

Explain your thinking:

Chapter 2 Quiz: Add To Change Unknown Problems

Solve with a model:

1. Lois left her house at 2:07 p.m. She went to the store and then to her friend's house. She came back at 4:35 p.m. How long was she gone?

2. The pizza shack had 18 kilos of shredded cheese. They got some more and now they have 40 kilos. How much shredded cheese did they get?

3. Troy ran 2/5 of a mile in the morning. In the afternoon, he ran some more. By the evening, he had run 4/5 of a mile. How far did he run in the afternoon?

4. Kelly had $55.67. She got some more money and now she has $82.69. How much money did she get?

CHAPTER 3
Add To Start Unknown Problems

In these problems students are looking for what happened in the beginning of the story. In this type of story we know what happened in the middle and we know how many we ended up with but we are looking for how the story started.

PROBLEM	John had some marbles. Henry gave him 7 more. Now he has 14. How many did he have in the beginning?
MODEL	+7 7 14
EQUATION	? + 7 = 14

ADD TO START UNKNOWN

1. Song A had several downloads from the internet in the morning. In the afternoon, Song A got 25,456 more downloads. Now it has 35,987 downloads all total. How many downloads did it have in the morning?

Way#1: Solve with numbers

Way#2: Check in a different way

Explain your thinking:

ADD TO START UNKNOWN

2. Erica went to the mall for 3 and a half hours. She then went to her friend's house for 1 hour and 15 minutes. She came back to her house at 4:15 p.m. What time did she leave her house originally?

Solve with a number line diagram

Explain your thinking:

ADD TO START UNKNOWN

3. Clarise ran in the morning. Then she ran ¼ mile more. All total she ran ½ of a mile. How far did she run in the morning.

Way#1: Solve with a drawing

Way#2: Solve with an equation, use a letter for the unknown

Explain your thinking:

Add to Start Unknown

4. Timothy had some money. For his birthday he got $45.44. Now he has $57.55. How much did he have in the beginning?

Way#1: Solve with an equation, use a letter for the unknown

Way#2: Check in a different way

Explain your thinking:

ADD TO START UNKNOWN

5. The school cook made some liters of fruit punch. He then made 15 more liters. Altogether he made 70 liters of fruit punch. How much fruit punch did he have in the beginning?

Way#1: Model with a drawing

Way#2: Solve with an equation, use a letter for the unknown

Explain your thinking:

Add to Start Unknown

6. Jay had some marbles. Tim gave him 23 more. His sister gave him 35 more. Now he has 70 marbles. How many marbles did he have to start with?

Way#1: Model with a tape diagram

Way#2: Solve with an equation, use a letter for the unknown

Explain your thinking:

ADD TO START UNKNOWN

7. The baker made some pies. He cut up several apples. Then he ran out of apples and needed some more. So, he cut up 3 ½ more cups of apples. In total, he cut up 5 cups of apples. How many cups did he cut up in the beginning?

Way#1: Solve with an illustration

Way#2: Solve with an equation, use a letter for the unknown

Explain your thinking:

ADD TO START UNKNOWN

8. Jonathan ran a bit in the morning. Then he ran 4/7 of a mile more. Altogether, he ran 6/7 of a mile. How much did he run in the morning?

Way#1: Solve with a number line

Way#2: Solve with an equation, use a letter for the unknown

Explain your thinking:

Chapter 3 Quiz: Add to Start Unknown Problems

Solve with a model:

1. Kelly had some string to make bracelets. She bought 89 more centimeters of string. Now she has 207 centimeters of string. How much string did she have in the beginning? How many meters of string does she have now?

2. Chung went to his grandmothers for 2 1/2 hours. Then he went to his cousin's house for another hour. He came home at 5:25. What time did he leave his house?

3. Chef Hong made a fancy soup. He put in some coconut juice and then he added 556 more ml of coconut juice. Altogether, he used 1023 ml of coconut juice. How much coconut juice did he have in the fancy soup in the beginning? Did he put in more than a liter altogether?

4. Steven ran on Monday morning. On Tuesday, he ran 2 more kilometers. On Wednesday, he ran another 3 kilometers. Altogether, he ran 8 kilometers. How many kilometers did he run on Monday morning?

Unit 1 Test: Addition Problems

Solve with a model:

1. The jewelry store had 100 rings. They got a shipment of 15 more on Monday, 59 more on Tuesday, and 46 more on Wednesday. How many rings do they have now?

2. Raul ran 1/6 of a mile in the morning, 2/6 of a mile in the afternoon and 3/6 of a mile in the evening. How far did Raul run? Did he run at least a mile?

3. Farmer Jen made a cage for her turtles. It was 4 feet long and 7 feet wide. What was the perimeter of the cage? What was the area of the cage?

4. Ichiro, the baker, made some fudge. He made some fudge to start with and then he made 849 more grams of it. He made 1 kilo of fudge altogether. How much did he make in the beginning?

CHAPTER 1
TAKE FROM RESULT UNKNOWN PROBLEMS

In these problems students are looking for what happened in the end of the story. In this type of story we know what happened at the beginning and also what change occurred. We are trying to find out how many things remained after some things were taken away.

PROBLEM	John had 10 apples. He gave 5 away. How many does he have left?
MODEL	-5 5 10
EQUATION	10 – ? = 5

TAKE FROM RESULT UNKNOWN

1. Daniel had $352. He paid $55 for some shoes, $38 for some videos, and $207 for some clothes. How much money did he have left?

Way#1: Solve with an open number line

Way#2: Solve with an equation, use a letter for the unknown

Explain your thinking:

TAKE FROM RESULT UNKNOWN

2. Baker Maria had 2 kilograms of cookies. She sold 234 grams in the morning, 612 grams in the afternoon and 908 grams in the evening. How many grams does she have left? Did she sell more than a kilogram of cookies?

Way#1: Model with a tape diagram

Way#2: Solve with an equation, use a letter for the unknown

Explain your thinking:

TAKE FROM RESULT UNKNOWN

3. Sara had 5 meters of wood. She needed 100 centimeters for each shelf that she was making. How many shelves could she make?

Way#1: Model with a table

Shelves	Centimeters	Meters
1	100	1

Way#2: Solve with an equation, use a letter for the unknown

Explain your thinking:

TAKE FROM RESULT UNKNOWN

4. Todd drank a pint of milk in the morning. He drank another pint in the afternoon and pint in the evening. How many ounces of milk did he drink? Did he drink at least a quart?

Way#1: Solve with a drawing

Way#2: Solve with an equation, use a letter for the unknown

Explain your thinking:

TAKE FROM RESULT UNKNOWN

5. Stephanie wanted to exercise for 2 hours. She spent 27 minutes on the treadmill, 45 minutes on the bicycle, and 15 minutes lifting weights. How many more minutes does she need to exercise to complete a 2 hour exercise routine?

Solve with an open number line diagram

Explain your thinking:

TAKE FROM RESULT UNKNOWN

6. The bakery sold 14 ounces of fudge in the morning, 5 ounces in the afternoon, and 8 ounces in the evening. How many ounces of fudge did they sell that day? Did they sell more than a pound?

Way#1: Model with a tape diagram

Way#2: Solve with an equation, use a letter for the unknown

Explain your thinking:

TAKE FROM RESULT UNKNOWN

7. Farmer Clark made a square cage for his chickens. The sides were 10 ft. long. The cage was too big, so he shortened the sides by 3 ft. each. How long was each new side? What is the new area and the new perimeter?

Way#1: Solve with a drawing

Way#2: Solve with the formulas for perimeter and area. Show all your work.

Explain your thinking:

TAKE FROM RESULT UNKNOWN

8. Grace wanted to run a mile. She ran ¼ of a mile in the morning and 2/4 of a mile in the afternoon. How far did she run? How much farther does she have to run to complete her 1-mile goal in the evening?

Way#1: Draw a picture to solve

Way#2: Solve with an equation, use a letter for the unknown

Explain your thinking:

Chapter 1 Quiz: Take From Result Unknown Problems

Solve with a model:

1. Joshua had $154. He spent $24 on games, $56 on shoes, and $59 on clothes. How much money did he have left?

2. The fruit stand had 2 kilos of apples. They sold 500 grams in the morning and 1000 more grams in the afternoon. How many grams of apples did they have left?

3. Lucinda had 2 meters of string. She used 78 centimeters to make a necklace and 55 centimeters to make a bracelet. How many centimeters of string did she have left? Does she have at least a meter left?

4. Fay had 3 hours to stay at the mall. She spent 90 minutes at the movies, 25 minutes in the arcade and 15 minutes in the candy store. How much time does she have left?

CHAPTER 2
TAKE FROM CHANGE UNKNOWN PROBLEMS

In these problems students are looking for what happened in the middle of the story. In this type of story we know what happened at the beginning but then some change happened and now we have less than we started with by the end of the story. We are trying to find out how many things were taken away in the middle of the story.

PROBLEM	John had 15 marbles. He gave some to his cousin. Now he has 12 left. How many did he give to his cousin?
MODEL	- 3 12 15
EQUATION	15 – ? = 12

Take from Change Unknown

1. Greg ran 2/3 of a mile in the morning. He ran some more in the afternoon. In total, he ran a mile. How far did he run in the afternoon?

Way#1: Solve with a number line

Way#2: Solve with an equation, use a letter for the unknown

Explain your thinking:

TAKE FROM CHANGE UNKNOWN

2. Lilia left her house at 3:15 p.m. She came back at 5:30 p.m. How long was she gone?

Solve with a number line diagram

Explain your thinking:

TAKE FROM CHANGE UNKNOWN

3. Tom the baker used 256 grams of sugar in his pie recipe. Then he used some more sugar for a cake. In total he used 302 grams of sugar. How many grams of sugar did he use for a cake?

Way#1: Model with a tape diagram

Way#2: Solve with an equation, use a letter for the unknown

Explain your thinking:

TAKE FROM CHANGE UNKNOWN

4. Grandma Betsy made a delicious fruit punch. She made 2 liters of punch. Her grandchildren drank 700 ml in the morning, 500 ml in the afternoon, and some more in the evening. At the end of the day, she had 235 ml left. How many more ml did her grandchildren drink in the evening?

Way#1: Model with a tape diagram

Way#2: Solve with an equation, use a letter for the unknown

Explain your thinking:

TAKE FROM CHANGE UNKNOWN

5. The store had 3 meters of string for sale. Customer 1 bought 125 cm, Customer 2 bought 107 cm, and Customer 3 bought some as well. Altogether, the store sold 280 cm of string. How much string did Customer Three buy? How many meters did the store sell?

Way#1: Solve with an open number line

Way#2: Solve with an equation, use a letter for the unknown

Explain your thinking:

TAKE FROM CHANGE UNKNOWN

6. The length of the fence was originally 12 ft. long. The width was 9 feet long. Dan shortened the fence. Now it is only 7 ft. long. By how much did Dan shorten the fence? What is the new perimeter? What is the new area?

Way#1: Solve with a drawing

Way#2: Solve with the formulas

Explain your thinking:

TAKE FROM CHANGE UNKNOWN

7. Kerry made a pizza. At first, he used 2/7 of a cup of yellow cheese. Then he added some more. Altogether, he used 5/7 cup of cheese on the pizza. How much cheese did he did he add to the pizza?

Way#1: Solve with an open number line

Way#2: Solve with an illustration

Explain your thinking:

TAKE FROM CHANGE UNKNOWN

8. Nancy had $405. She spent $105 on shoes, $227 on clothes, and some more money on jewelry. She spent $380. How much did she spend on jewelry? How much does she have left?

Way#1: Model with a tape diagram

Way#2: Solve with an equation, use a letter for the unknown

Explain your thinking:

Chapter 2 Quiz: Take from Change Unknown Problems

Solve with a model:

1. Mark had 87 trading cards. He gave 15 to his brother, 18 to his cousin, and some to his friend. He gave a total of 42 trading cards away. How many trading cards did he give to his friend? How many does he have left?

2. Baker Daniel had 3 pounds of butter. He used 9 ounces for some cookies, 8 ounces for some cakes, and 7 ounces for some pies. How many ounces of butter did he have left?

3. Mr. Vega left his house at 2:17 p.m. He came back at 5:02 p.m. How long was he gone?

4. Tamara had $91. She spent $27 on jewelry, $28 on clothes, and some more money on shoes. She spent $82 in all. How much did she spend on shoes? How much did she have left?

CHAPTER 3
TAKE FROM START UNKNOWN PROBLEMS

In these problems students are looking for how many things there were at the beginning of the story. In this type of story we only know that there was some amount and that there was a change (some things were taken away). We know what was taken away and how much was left. We are trying to find out how much we had in the beginning of the story.

PROBLEM	John had some marbles. He gave his brother 5. Now he has 10 left. How many did he have in the beginning?
MODEL	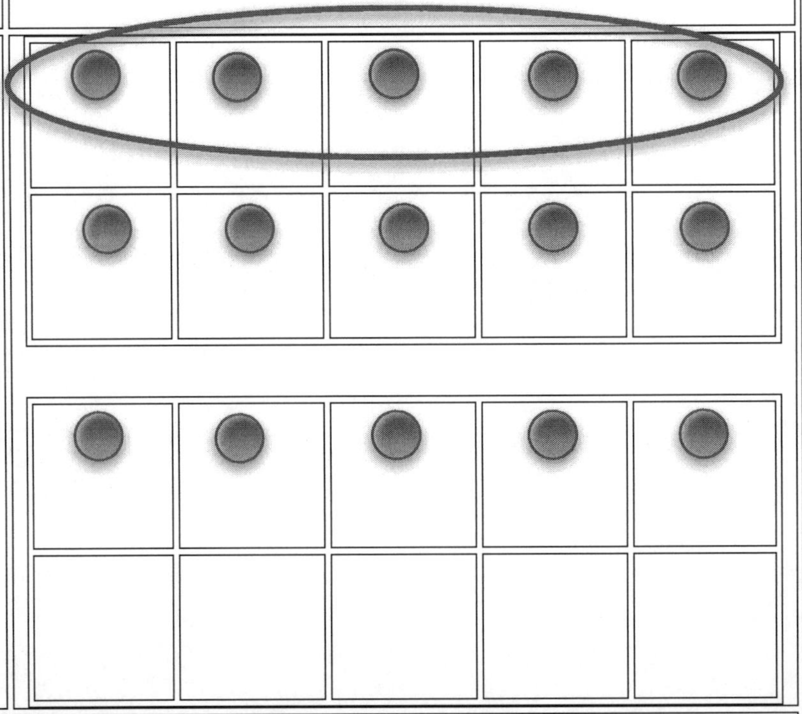
EQUATION	? - 5 = 10 15 - 5 = 10

TAKE FROM START UNKNOWN

1. Taylor spent $45 on shoes, $86 on clothes, and $48 on jewelry. She had $19 left. How much money did she have in the beginning?

Way#1: Solve with an open number line

Way#2: Solve with an equation, use a letter for the unknown

Explain your thinking:

TAKE FROM START UNKNOWN

2. Grandpa Ben drank some milk in the morning. He drank 450 ml of milk in the afternoon and 289 of milk in the evening. Altogether he drank 900 ml of milk. How much milk did he drink in the morning?

Way#1: Solve with a drawing

Way#2: Solve with an equation, use a letter for the unknown

Explain your thinking:

TAKE FROM START UNKNOWN

3. Grandma Betsy baked all morning. She used some flour for her cake, 350 grams of flour for her pies, and 276 grams of flour for her cookies. She used 1 kilogram of flour in total. How many grams of flour did she use for her cake?

Way#1: Solve with a tape diagram

Way#2: Solve with an equation, use a letter for the unknown

Explain your thinking:

Take from Start Unknown

4. Mary ate some pizza for lunch. She ate 2/4 of a pizza for dinner. She ate a total of ¾ of a pizza. How much pizza did she have for lunch?

Way#1: Solve with a number line

Way#2: Solve with an illustration

Explain your thinking:

TAKE FROM START UNKNOWN

5. Carlos had some marbles. He gave Jose 9 marbles. He gave his brother 12 marbles. Now he has 56 marbles left. How many marbles did he have to start with?

Way#1: Model with a tape diagram

Way#2: Solve with numbers

Explain your thinking:

TAKE FROM START UNKNOWN

6. Jessica had some string. She used 24 inches to make a necklace, 18 inches to make a bracelet, and 3 inches to make a ring. She had 15 inches of string left. How much string did she have in the beginning? Did she use more than a yard to make her jewelry?

Way#1: Solve with a tape diagram

Way#2: Solve with numbers

Explain your thinking:

TAKE FROM START UNKNOWN

7. Clint left his house early. He went to the store for 45 minutes. Then he went to his friend's house for 1 hour. Finally, he went to the park for 10 minutes. He got home at 3:15 p.m. What time did he leave his house?

Solve with a number line diagram

Explain your thinking:

TAKE FROM START UNKNOWN

8. Mike drank some orange juice in the morning. He drank 450 ml in the afternoon. He drank 489 more in the evening. Altogether, he drank 1078 ml of orange juice. How much orange juice did he drink in the morning? Did he drink more than a liter?

Way#1: Solve with a tape diagram

Way#2: Solve with numbers

Explain your thinking:

Chapter 3 Quiz: Take from Start Unknown Problems

Solve with a model:

1. On Monday, some people listened to Song A. On Tuesday, 2,345,687 more people listened to Song A. By Wednesday morning, 3,456,909 people had listened to Song A. How many people had listened to Song A on Monday?

2. Ben ran in the morning. In the afternoon, he ran 2/5 of a mile more. By the evening, he ran 5/5 of a mile. How far had he run in the morning?

3. The candy store sold some chocolate in the morning. In the afternoon, they sold 500 more grams of it. In total, they sold 1 kilogram of chocolate. How much did they sell in the morning?

4. Mr. Griggs had some money. He spent $149 on shoes, $40 on a tie, $28 on a wallet, and $367 on clothes. He had $17 left. How much money did he have in the beginning?

Unit 2 Test:
Take from Problems

Solve with a model:

1. Manny had a small pizza. He at 1/8 of the pizza in the morning and 2/8 of the pizza in the afternoon. He ate 3/8 of the pizza in the evening. How much pizza did he eat altogether?

2. Hallie had some money. She spent $167 on jewelry, $78 on shoes, $109 on clothes, and $16 on candy. She has $35 left. How much did she have in the beginning?

3. Grandma Mabel had 500 grams of sugar. She used 349 grams in her cookies. Then she used some more for muffins. In total, she used 475 grams of sugar. How much sugar did she use for the muffins? How much did she have left?

4. Kelly arrived at the mall at 3:10 p.m. She left her house 25 minutes earlier. What time did she leave her house?

CHAPTER 1
PUT TOGETHER/TAKE APART PROBLEMS

These types of problems are about sets of things. In them we know both parts and we are looking for the whole. What distinguishes a Put Together/Take Apart Problem from an Add to Result Unknown problem is action. In a Put together/Take Apart Problem there is no action, only a set of something.

PROBLEM	John had five red apples and five green ones. How many apples did he have altogether?
MODEL	
EQUATION	5 + 5 = 10

PUT TOGETHER/TAKE APART—WHOLE UNKNOWN

1. This weekend in our city, 46,345 people went to see Movie A. There were a total of 29,999 people that went to see Movie B. How many people went to see these two movies?

Way#1: Solve using any method

Way#2: Check your answer in a different way

Explain your thinking:

PUT TOGETHER/TAKE APART - WHOLE UNKNOWN

2. Sue built a fence. The length was 8 ft. The width was 5 ft. What was the perimeter? What was the area?

Way#1: Solve with a drawing

Way#2: Solve with the formulas

Explain your thinking:

PUT TOGETHER/TAKE APART—WHOLE UNKNOWN

3. John and his math partner were trying to solve an angle problem. They knew that one angle was 50 degrees, the other was 80 degrees and the other was 50. What was the total number of degrees of the angles in the triangle?

Solve with a number line diagram

Explain your thinking:

PUT TOGETHER/TAKE APART - WHOLE UNKNOWN

4. Sue biked 1/6 of a mile in the morning, 2/6 of a mile in the afternoon, and 3/6 of a mile in the evening. How far did Sue bike altogether? Did she bike at least a mile?

Way#1: Solve with a number line

Way#2: Solve with an equation, use a letter for the unknown

Explain your thinking:

Put Together/Take Apart—Whole Unknown

5. Grandma Betsy used 378 grams of sugar in her first pie, 234 grams in her second, and 698 grams in her third. How many grams of sugar did she use in her pies? Did she use more or less than a kilogram of sugar?

Way#1: Solve with a tape diagram

Way#2: Solve with an equation, use a letter for the unknown

Explain your thinking:

PUT TOGETHER/TAKE APART—WHOLE UNKNOWN

6. Sue left her house at 2:10 p.m. She spent 45 minutes at her aunt's house and 45 minutes at her grandmother's house. How long was she out visiting? What time did she get back home?

Solve with an open number line diagram

Explain your thinking:

PUT TOGETHER/TAKE APART - WHOLE UNKNOWN

7. Grandpa Raul made a fruit punch for his grandkids. He used 1 liter of pineapple juice, 500 ml of apple juice, 359 ml of grape juice, and 876 ml of orange juice. How many milliliters of fruit punch did he make? How many liters of fruit punch did he make?

Way#1: Solve with a tape diagram

Way#2: Solve with numbers

Explain your thinking:

Put Together/Take Apart—Whole Unknown

8. Macy wanted to exercise for 1 hour. She spent 23 minutes on the bike, 19 minutes on the treadmill, and 20 minutes weight lifting. How many minutes did she exercise? Did she complete an hour of exercise?

Way#1: Solve with an open number line

Way#2: Solve with an equation, use a letter for the unknown

Explain your thinking:

Chapter 1 Quiz: Put Together/ Take Apart – Whole Unknown Problems

Solve with a model:

1. Tom's grandpa gave him 4/10 of a dollar. His grandma gave him 50/100 of a dollar. How much money did they give him in total?

2. The candy store made some fudge. They made 234 grams of chocolate fudge, 457 grams of vanilla fudge, and 420 grams of peanut butter fudge. How many grams of fudge did they make altogether? Did they make more or less than a kilogram of fudge?

3. Kayla got some money for her birthday. Her grandma gave her $21.80. Her dad gave her $15.00. Her sister gave her $17.10. How much did she get for her birthday?

4. Chef Hugo used 1 kilogram of chocolate to bake. He then used another 500 grams of chocolate to make a sauce for his chicken. How many grams of chocolate did he use altogether?

CHAPTER 2
PUT TOGETHER/TAKE APART PROBLEMS PART UNKNOWN

These types of problems are about sets of things. In them we know the total and one part of the set. We are looking for the other part of the set.

PROBLEM	John had ten apples. Five were red apples and the rest were green. How many apples were green?
MODEL	+5 5 10
EQUATION	5 + 5 = 10

PUT TOGETHER/TAKE APART - PART UNKNOWN

1. The fruit stand had 100 apples. Half of them were red and the other half green. How many were green?

Way#1: Solve with a number line

Way#2: Solve with an equation, use a letter for the unknown

Explain your thinking:

PUT TOGETHER/TAKE APART - PART UNKNOWN

2. Tina spent \$498. She spent \$273 on clothes, \$99 on shoes, \$28 on jewelry and the rest on perfume. How much did she spend on perfume?

Way#1: Model with a tape diagram

Way#2: Solve with numbers

Explain your thinking:

PUT TOGETHER/TAKE APART - PART UNKNOWN

3. Twenty thousand people went to the movies this weekend. 7,349 people went to see comedies. 8,459 people went to see horror movies and the rest went to see action movies. How many people went to see action movies?

Way#1: Solve with numbers

Way#2: Check your answer a different way

Explain your thinking:

PUT TOGETHER/TAKE APART - PART UNKNOWN

4. The farm had 12 rabbits. One-fourth of them were black, one-fourth of them were white, and the rest were brown. What fraction of the rabbits were brown? How many were brown?

Way#1: Solve with a drawing

Way#2: Solve with an equation, use a letter for the unknown

Explain your thinking:

PUT TOGETHER/TAKE APART - PART UNKNOWN

5. Jamal and his partner were working on a math problem. They were looking at a triangle. They knew that one angle measured 25 degrees and the other measured 75 degrees. How much did the 3rd angle measure?

Solve with a number line

Explain your thinking:

PUT TOGETHER/TAKE APART—PART UNKNOWN

6. Grandma Betsy used 1 kilogram of sugar for her cookies. She used 456 grams in her sugar cookies and the rest in her chocolate chip cookies. How many grams of sugar did she use in her chocolate chip cookies?

Way#1: Model with a tape diagram

Way#2: Solve with numbers

Explain your thinking:

PUT TOGETHER/TAKE APART - PART UNKNOWN

7. Anna made 2 liters of fruit punch. She used 800 ml of orange juice, 203 ml of pineapple juice, 259 ml of apple juice, and 175 ml of cherry juice. The rest of the fruit punch was banana juice. How many ml was banana juice?

Way#1: Model with a tape diagram

Way#2: Solve with an equation, use a letter for the unknown

Explain your thinking:

PUT TOGETHER/TAKE APART - PART UNKNOWN

8. Jimmy built a rectangular fence with a perimeter of 30 ft. The length was 10 feet. What was the width? What was the area?

Way#1: Model with a drawing

Way#2: Solve using the formula for area

Explain your thinking:

Chapter 2 Quiz: Put Together/Take Apart - Part Unknown

Solve with a model.

1. Dana had $456. She spent $88 on earrings, $43 on necklaces, $235 on clothes, and the rest on shoes. How much did she spend on shoes?

2. Chef Sue made a pie. She used 500 grams of sugar. She used 345 grams of white sugar and the rest was brown sugar. How much brown sugar did she use?

3. John drank 1 liter of apple juice. He drank 146 ml in the morning, 256 ml in the afternoon, and the rest in the evening. How many ml did he drink in the evening?

4. Jackson cut 3 meters of wood. First, he cut 59 centimeters, then he cut another 128 centimeters, and then he cut the rest. How many more centimeters of wood did he cut?

UNIT 3 TEST
PUT TOGETHER/TAKE APART TEST

Solve with a model.

1. Farmer Jamie is building a pen for his chickens. The original pen was 8 feet long and 9 feet wide. He realized that it was too small. So he added 3 feet to the length. What is the length of the new pen? What is the perimeter of the new pen? What is the area of the new pen?

2. Chris ran 2 miles. He ran 5/8 of a mile in the morning, 7/8 of a mile in the afternoon and the rest in the evening. How far did he run in the evening?

3. Mom and Julie are making some baked items for the school bake sale. They use 360 grams of sugar in their cupcakes and twice as much in a large cake. How much sugar did they use in the cake? How much sugar did they use altogether?

4. The trip from Sam's house to the library is one mile. On the way, he passes a school and a firehouse. From his house to the school it's 2/8 of a mile. From the school to the firehouse it's another 5/8 of a mile. Next stop is the library. How far is it from the firehouse to the library?

CHAPTER 1
COMPARE DIFFERENCE UNKNOWN

In these problems students are comparing two or more amounts. They are comparing to find out what is the difference between the amounts. There are two versions of this type of story. One version uses the word more and one version uses the word fewer. The version with the word fewer is more difficult.

PROBLEM MORE VERSION	John had 12 marbles. Carl had 2 marbles. How many more marbles does John have than Carl?
MODEL	John Carl Difference is 10 2 12
EQUATION	2 + ? = 12 2 + 10 =12

PROBLEM FEWER VERSION	Carl had 2 marbles. John had 12 marbles. How many fewer marbles does Carl have than John?
MODEL	John Carl
EQUATION	12 – 2 =? 12 – 2 = 10

COMPARE FRACTIONS

1. Tim ate 2/3 of a small pizza. Clark ate 1/3 of a small pizza. How much more pizza did Tim eat than Clark?

Way#1: Solve with pictures

Way#2: Solve with a number line

Explain your thinking:

COMPARE FRACTIONS

2. Tommy ate 5/6 of his candy bar. Kayla at 6/6 of hers. If the candy bars were the same size, who ate more?

Way#1: Solve with a number line

Way#2: Show the relationship with the symbols <, >, or =

Explain your thinking:

COMPARE FRACTIONS

3. Jose jogged 2/4 of a mile this morning. Tom jogged 1/2 of a mile this afternoon. Who ran farther?

Way#1: Solve with an illustration

Way#2: Solve with a number line

Explain your thinking:

COMPARE USING LINE PLOTS

4. Here are the lengths (in feet) of several pieces of string that were cut.

1/8, 1/8, 2/8, 3/8, 3/8, 3/8, 4/8, 1/2, 1/2,1/2, 1/2,1/2

Make a line plot for the data

Question 1: What was the total amount of the 1/8 ft. ribbons cut?

Question 2: What was the difference between the shortest and longest ribbons?

COMPARE USING LINE PLOT

5. These are the lengths (in inches) of various flowers that grew in the garden last week.

1/4, 1/4, 1/4, 2/4, 2/4, 2/4, 3/4, 3/4, 3/4, 3/4, 3/4

Make a line plot for the data

Question 1: What is the total length of the flowers that grew 2/4 of an inch?

Question 2: What is the difference between the shortest length and the tallest length that the flowers grew?

COMPARE DIFFERENCE UNKNOWN

6. Susie had \$0.60 and Don had \$0.55. Who had more money? How much more?

Way#1: Illustrate with money

Way#2: Compare the decimals with symbols <,>, or =

Explain your thinking:

COMPARE DIFFERENCE UNKNOWN

7. In one hour, on the internet 7,500 people like Video A, but only 2,578 people liked Video B. How many more people liked Video A than liked Video B? How many people liked for the videos altogether?

Way#1: Solve with numbers

Way#2: Record the results of comparisons with symbols <, >, or = and justify with a model

Explain your thinking:

COMPARE DIFFERENCE UNKNOWN

8. Mara drew an acute angle. Carol drew a right angle. Whose angle was larger?

Way#1: Solve with an illustration

Way#2: Compare with symbols

Explain your thinking:

Chapter 1 Quiz: Compare Problems

Solve with a model:

1. In 1 hour, 4,908 people voted for Song A on the internet. Only 3,999 people voted for Song B. How many fewer people voted for Song B than liked Song A? How many people voted altogether?

2. John had 50/100 of a dollar. Tom had 6/10 of a dollar. Who had more? How much more?

3. Chef Juan used 567 grams of sugar for his sweet potato pie and 489 grams of sugar for his pineapple cake. How much less sugar did he use for his pineapple cake than for his sweet potato pie?

4. Kayla ate 1/5 of her candy bar. Luke at 5/5 of his candy bar. If the candy bars were the same size, who ate more? How much more?

CHAPTER 2
COMPARISON – BIGGER PART UNKNOWN

In these problems students are comparing two or more amounts. They are comparing to find out who had the bigger part. There are two versions of this type of story. One version uses the word more and one version uses the word fewer. The version with the word *fewer* is considered to be more difficult.

PROBLEM MORE VERSION	John has 5 more marbles than Carl. Carl has 2 marbles. How many marbles does John have?
MODEL	7 total John Carl
EQUATION	2 + 5 = ? 2 + 5 = 7

PROBLEM FEWER VERSION	Carl has 3 fewer marbles than John? Carl has 2 marbles. How many marbles does John have?
MODEL	Carl John 5 total
	2 + 3 = ? 2 + 3 = 5

COMPARISON – BIGGER PART UNKNOWN

1. The candy store sold 459 grams of chocolate fudge. It sold 379 more grams of strawberry swirl fudge. How much strawberry swirl fudge did it sell?

Way#1: Solve with a double number line

Way#2: Record the results of comparisons with symbols <, >, or = and justify with a model

Explain your thinking:

COMPARISON – BIGGER PART UNKNOWN

2. Grandpa Ben used 289 grams of sugar in his apple pie and 240 more grams of sugar in his pineapple cake. How many grams of sugar did he use in his pineapple cake?

Way#1: Model with a tape diagram

Way#2: Record the results of comparisons with symbols <, >, or = and justify with a model

Explain your thinking:

COMPARISON – BIGGER PART UNKNOWN

3. Emily drank 2 pints of orange juice. Carol drank 2 more pints of orange juice than Emily did. How many more cups of orange juice did Carol drink than Emily? Did Carol drink a quart of orange juice?

Way#1: Solve with pictures

Way#2: Record the results of comparisons with symbols <, >, or = and justify with a model

Explain your thinking:

COMPARISON – BIGGER PART UNKNOWN

4. Jonathan drank 398 ml of milk in the morning. Jamal drank 349 more ml of milk than Jonathan. Did he drink more or less than a liter or milk?

Way#1: Solve with an illustration

Way#2: Record the results of comparisons with symbols <, >, or = and justify with a model

Explain your thinking:

COMPARISON – BIGGER PART UNKNOWN

5. Miguel had $23.45. Luke had $10.40 more than Miguel did. How much money did Luke have?

Way#1: Solve with numbers

Way#2: Record the results of comparisons with symbols <, >, or = and justify with a model

Explain your thinking:

COMPARISON – BIGGER PART UNKNOWN

6. Yanni ran ¼ of a mile. Luke ran 2/4 of a mile farther than Yanni. How far did Luke run?

Way#1: Solve with a double number line

Way#2: Record the results of comparisons with symbols <, >, or = and justify with a model

Explain your thinking:

COMPARISON – BIGGER PART UNKNOWN

7. The toy store has 89 red marbles, 34 multicolored marbles, and 56 black marbles. There are ten more green marbles than black marbles. There are twenty more purple marbles than the red and multicolored marbles combined. How many green marbles are there? How many purple marbles are there? How many marbles are there altogether?

Way#1: Model with a tape diagram

Way#2: Solve with numbers

Explain your thinking:

COMPARISON – BIGGER PART UNKNOWN

8. Carl drank 856 ml of orange juice. He drank 78 fewer ml fewer than Ricky. How many ml of orange juice did Ricky drink?

Way#1: Solve with a double number line

Way#2: Record the results of comparisons with symbols <, >, or = and justify with a model

Explain your thinking:

Chapter 2 Quiz: Compare Bigger Part Unknown

Solve with a model:

1. Mark at 2/12 of his candy bar. Miguel at 6/12 more of his candy bar than Mark did of his. The candy bars were the same size. How much of his candy bar did Miguel eat?

2. Song A has 28,345 votes. It has 3,500 fewer votes than Song B. How many votes does Song B have?

3. The bakery used 589 grams of sugar for cookies. It used 378 more grams of sugar for doughnuts than for cookies. How many grams of sugar did it use for doughnuts? How many grams of sugar did it use altogether?

4. Harry drank 508 ml of milk. His brother drank 100 more ml than he did. His cousin drank 358 more ml than his brother did. How much did his brother drink? How much did his cousin drink? Did anyone drink more than a liter? If so, who?

CHAPTER 3
COMPARISON – SMALLER PART UNKNOWN

In these problems students are comparing two or more amounts. They are comparing to find out who has the smaller amount. There are two versions of this type of story. One version uses the word more and one version uses the word fewer. The version with the word *more* is considered to be more difficult.

PROBLEM MORE VERSION	John had 4 more marbles than Carl. John had 5 marbles. How many marbles did Carl have?
MODEL	John Carl
EQUATION	5 – 4 = ? 5 – 4 =1

PROBLEM FEWER VERSION	Carl had 10 fewer marbles than John. John had 12 marbles. How many marbles did Carl have?
MODEL	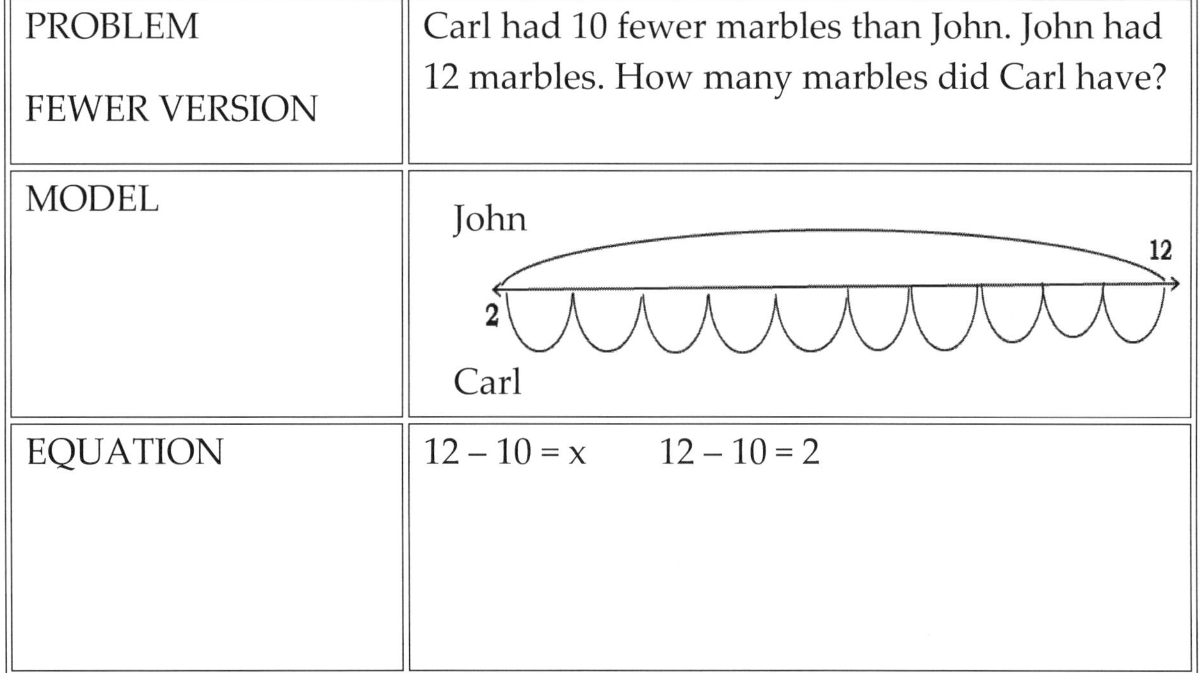 John 12 2 Carl
EQUATION	12 – 10 = x 12 – 10 = 2

COMPARISON – SMALLER PART UNKNOWN

1. Luke ate 2/4 of a candy bar. John ate ¼ less than Luke did. The candy bars were the same size. How much of the candy bar did John eat?

Way#1: Solve with a double number line

Way#2: Solve with an equation, use a letter for the unknown

Explain your thinking:

COMPARISON – SMALLER PART UNKNOWN

2. Becky made some cookies. She put 456 grams of flour in the chocolate chip cookies. She put 100 more grams of flour in the chocolate chip cookies than in the peanut butter cookies. How much flour did she put in the peanut butter cookies?

Way#1: Model with a tape diagram

Way#2: Solve with an equation, use a letter for the unknown

Explain your thinking:

COMPARISON – SMALLER PART UNKNOWN

3. Song A has 15,299 downloads. Song B has 1,645 fewer downloads than Song A. How many downloads does Song B have?

Way#1: Solve with numbers

Way#2: Check a different way

Explain your thinking:

COMPARISON – SMALLER PART UNKNOWN

4. Lucy made a great fruit punch. She used 345 ml of pineapple juice and 204 fewer ml of apple juice. How much apple juice did she use?

Way#1: Solve with drawing

Way#2: Solve with an equation, use a letter for the unknown

Explain your thinking:

COMPARISON – SMALLER PART UNKNOWN

5. Mr. Robinson planted 2 gardens. Garden A had a length of 6 ft. and a width of 7 ft. The length of Garden B was 1 ft. smaller than the length of Garden A and the width of Garden B was 2 ft. smaller than the width of Garden A. What was the perimeter of Garden A? What was the perimeter of Garden B?

Way#1: Model with a drawing

Way#2: Solve using the formulas for area and perimeter

Explain your thinking:

COMPARISON – SMALLER PART UNKNOWN

6. Henry had $45.76. His brother had $22.50 less than Henry. How much money did Henry's brother have?

Way#1: Solve with numbers

Way#2: Check in a different way

Explain your thinking:

COMPARISON – SMALLER PART UNKNOWN

7. Chef Luke used 1 lb. of butter in his special bread. He used 5 fewer ounces of butter in his pasta. How many ounces of butter did he use in his pasta?

Way #1: Model with a tape diagram

Way #2: Solve with numbers

Explain your thinking:

Comparison – Smaller Part Unknown

8. Luke cut 3 meters of wood. Hank cut 100 fewer cm than Luke did. How much wood did Hank cut?

Way#1: Model with a tape diagram

Way#2: Solve with numbers

Explain your thinking:

Chapter 3 Quiz: Compare Smaller Unknown Problems

Solve with a model:

1. The jewelry store had 145 silver rings. They had 34 fewer gold rings than silver ones. They had 10 fewer wooden rings than gold ones. How many gold rings did they have? How many wooden rings did they have?

2. Mrs. Thomas planted 2 gardens. Garden A was had a square perimeter of 24 ft. Garden B had a length 2 feet shorter than Garden A and a width 3 ft. shorter than Garden A. What was the perimeter of Garden B?

3. Raul ran 3/4 of a mile. Frank ran 1/4 of a mile less than Raul. How far did Frank run?

4. Sue had 4 meters of string. Ann had 200 fewer centimeters of string than Sue. How much string did Ann have?

Unit 4 Test: Compare Problems

Solve with a model:

1. Kate ate 2/4 of her candy bar. Joe ate 3/4 of his. If the candy bars were the same size, who ate more? How much more?

2. Grandma Lily used 345 grams of flour in her lemon cake. She used 200 more grams of sugar in her peach cake than in her lemon cake. How many grams did she use in her peach cake? How many grams of sugar did she use for both cakes?

3. Joe ran 2/4 of a mile. John ran 1/4 of a mile more than Joe. Luke ran ¼ of a mile less than Joe. How far did John run? How far did Luke run? How far did they run altogether?

4. Mary went shopping. She spent $123 on perfume. She spent $100 more on a scarf than she did on perfume. She spent $20 less on earrings than she did on the scarf. How much did the scarf cost? How much did the earrings cost?

Final Word Problem Test

Fourth Grade

NAME:

DATE:

Solve the problems. Show your work by drawing a picture, using a number line, making a table, or using formulas.

1. Larry left his house at 5:15 p.m. He spent an hour and 15 minutes at Brian's house and an hour and a half at the basketball court. What time did he go home?

2. Don, the baker, used 25 grams of sugar in his cake mixture. Then he added 37 more grams of sugar. How many grams of sugar did he use for his cake?

3. Farmer Jane built a yard for her rabbits. First, she made a yard that was 8ft long and 9 ft. wide. Then she added some length to the fence. Now the length is 12 ft. long. How many feet did she add to the length? What is the new perimeter of the yard?

4. The school cook made some liters of fruit punch. He then made 4 more liters. Altogether, he made 20 liters of fruit punch. How much fruit punch did he make in the beginning?

5. Sara had 205 cm of string to make bracelets. She used 88 cm on Monday, 26 cm on Tuesday, 28 cm on Wednesday, and 14 cm on Thursday. How much string did she have left on Friday?

6. John left his house at 2:15 p.m. He came back at 5:55 p.m. How long was he gone?

7. The candy store sold 900 grams of chocolate in the morning, 180 grams in the afternoon, and some more in the evening. Altogether, they sold 2 kilograms of chocolate. How much did they sell in the evening?

8. Carl cooked all morning. He used some butter in the soup. In his bread, he used 12 more ounces of butter. In total, he used 1 pound of butter. How much butter did he put in the soup?

9. Ten thousand people went to the movies this weekend in our city. All total, 5,759 people went to see comedies, 3,489 people went to see dramas, and the rest went to see action movies. How many people went to see action movies?

10. Justin built a fence with a perimeter of 48 ft. The length was 12 feet. What was the width?

11. Tommy ate 1/6 of his candy bar. Kayla ate 5/6 of hers. If the candy bars were the same size, who ate more? How much more?

12. Paco used 140 ml of apple juice in his punch and 200 more ml of orange juice than apple juice. How much orange juice did he use?

13. Lucia's class cut several strips of ribbon. Here is the data (in inches) of the sizes.

3/4, 3/4, 3/4, 3/4, 3/4, 1/4, 1/4, 1/4, 1/4, 2/4, 2/4, 2/4, 2/4

Make a line plot

Question 1: How many people cut 3/4?

Question 2: How many people cut 1/4 inch of ribbon?

Question 3: How many people cut 1/2 an inch?

14. On the internet Song A got 15,991 votes in 1 hour. Song B got 2,347 fewer votes than Song A. How many votes did Song B get? How many people voted altogether?

15. John drew an acute angle and Clark drew an obtuse angle. Whose angle is larger?

Answer Key

Unit 1
Add to Problems

Chapter 1: Add to Result Unknown Problems

1. 52,844 downloads
2. 1 hour, 10 minutes
3. 1,085 grams; yes
4. 934 ml; no
5. $154.30
6. No, he ran exactly a mile
7. 46 ft.; 112 ft.
8.

Necklaces	Inches	Feet
1	12	1
2	24	2
3	36	3

Chapter 1 Quiz: Add to Result Unknown

1. 3 quarts; no
2. 30 ft.; 56 square ft.
3. 1,043 meters; yes
4. 9/6 or 1 ½ yards; yes

Chapter 2: Add to Change Unknown Problems

1. 565 grams; yes
2. 1 hour, 52 minutes
3. 3/6 or ½ of a mile
4. 600 ml of apple juice
5. $17.05
6. 45 centimeters
7. 6 ft.; 34 ft.
8. 13 ounces

Chapter 2 Quiz: Add to Change Unknown Problem

1. 2 hours, 28 minutes
2. 22 kilos
3. 2/5 of a mile
4. $27.02

Chapter 3: Add to Start Unknown

1. 10,531 downloads
2. 11:30
3. ¼ mile
4. $12.11
5. 55 liters
6. 12 marbles
7. 1 ½ cups of apples
8. 2/7 of a mile

Chapter 3 Quiz: Add to Start Unknown Problems

1. 118 centimeters; 1 meter, 18 cm
2. 1:55
3. 467 ml; yes
4. 3 kilometers

UNIT 1 TEST: ADDITION PROBLEMS

1. 220 rings
2. 6/6 or 1 mile; yes
3. 22 ft.; 28 square feet
4. 151 grams;

ANSWER KEY

Unit 2
Take From Problems

Chapter 1: Take From Result Unknown

1. $52
2. 246 grams; yes
3.

Shelves	Centimeters	Meters
1	100	1
2	200	2
3	300	3
4	400	4
5	500	5

4. 48 ounces; yes
5. 33 more minutes
6. 27 ounces; yes
7. 7 ft.; 49 square ft.; 28 ft.
8. ¾ of a mile; ¼ of mile farther

Chapter 1 Quiz: Take From Result Unknown Problems

1. $15
2. 500 grams
3. 67 centimeters; no
4. 50 min.

Chapter 2: Take From Change Unknown Problems

1. 1/3 of a mile
2. 2 hours, 15 minutes
3. 46 grams of sugar
4. 565 ml
5. 58 cm; 2 meters, 80 cm
6. 10 ft.; 32 ft.; 63 square ft.
7. 3/7 of a cup
8. $48; $25

Chapter 2 Quiz: Take From Change Unknown Problems

1. 9 trading cards; 45 left
2. 24 ounces
3. 2 hours, 45 minutes
4. $27; $9

Chapter 3: Take From Start Unknown Problems

1. $198
2. 161 ml
3. 374 grams
4. ¼ of the pizza
5. 77 marbles
6. 60 inches; yes
7. 1:20
8. 139 ml; yes

Chapter 3 Quiz: Take From Start Unknown Problems

1. 1,111,222 people
2. 3/5 of a mile
3. 500 grams
4. $601

UNIT 2 TEST: TAKE FROM PROBLEMS

1. 6/8 or ¾ of the pizza
2. $405
3. 126 grams; 25 grams
4. 2:45

Answer Key

Unit 3
Put Together/Take Apart Problems

Chapter 1: Put Together/Take Apart—Whole Unknown Problems

1. 76,344 people
2. 26 ft.; 40 square feet
3. 180 degrees
4. 6/6 of a mile or 1 mile; yes
5. 1,310 grams; more than a kilogram
6. 1 hour, 30 minutes; 3:40
7. 2,735 ml; 2 liters, 735 ml
8. 62 minutes; yes

Chapter 1 Quiz: Put Together/Take Apart—Whole Unknown Problems

1. 90 cents
2. 1,111 grams; more than a kilogram
3. $53.90
4. 1500 grams

Chapter 2: Put Together/Take Apart—Part Unknown Problems

1. 50 green apples
2. $98
3. 4,192 people
4. 6 rabbits
5. 80 degrees
6. 544 grams
7. 563 ml
8. 5 ft.; 50 square feet

Chapter 2 Quiz: Put Together/Take Apart—Part Unknown Problems

1. $90
2. 155 grams
3. 598 ml
4. 113 centimeters

UNIT 3 TEST: PUT TOGETHER/TAKE APART PROBLEMS

1. 11 ft.; 40 ft.; 99 square ft.
2. 4/8 of a mile
3. 720 grams; 1,080 grams
4. 1/8 of a mile

Unit 4
Comparison - Difference Unknown Problems

Chapter 1: Compare Fraction Problems

1. 1/3 more of the pizza
2. Kayla
3. They ran the same distance
4. 2/8 or ¼ feet; 3/8 of a foot
5. 6/4 or 1 2/4 or 1 ½ inches; 2/4 or ½ an inch
6. Susie; $0.05 more
7. 4,922 more people; 10,078 people voted
8. Carl's angle

Chapter 1 Quiz: Compare Problems

1. 909 fewer people; 8,907 people voted
2. Tom; 10 cents more
3. 78 fewer grams
4. Luke; 4/5 more

Answer Key

Chapter 2: Comparison—Bigger Part Unknown Problems

1. 838 grams
2. 529 grams
3. 4 more cups; yes
4. 747 ml; less
5. $33.85
6. ¾ of a mile
7. 66 green marbles; 143 purple marbles; 388 marbles in all
8. 934 ml

Chapter 2 Quiz: Comparison—Bigger Part Unknown Problems

1. 8/12 or 2/3 of the candy bar
2. 31,845 votes
3. 967 grams; 1556 g
4. 608 ml; 966 ml; no

Chapter 3: Comparison—Smaller Part Unknown Problems

1. ¼ of the candy bar
2. 356 grams
3. 13,654 downloads
4. 141 ml
5. 26 ft.; 20 ft.
6. $23.26
7. 11 ounces
8. 200 centimeters or 2 meters

Chapter 3 Quiz: Comparison Smaller Unknown Problems

1. 111 gold rings; 101 wooden rings
2. 14 ft.
3. 2/4 or ½ of a mile
4. 200 centimeters or 2 meters

UNIT 4 TEST: COMPARE PROBLEMS

1. Joe; ¼ more
2. 545 grams; 890 grams
3. ¾; ¼; 6/4 or 1 ½ miles
4. $223; $203

Final Word Problem Test

1. 8:00
2. 62 grams
3. 4 ft.; 42 ft.
4. 16 liters
5. 49 cm
6. 3 hours, 40 minutes
7. 920 grams
8. 4 ounces
9. 752 people
10. 12 feet
11. Kayla; 4/6 more
12. 340 ml
13. 5; 4; 4
14. 13.644 votes; 29,635 people voted
15. Clark's angle is larger

REFERENCES

Charles, R. *Solving Word Problems: Developing Students' Quantitative Reasoning Abilities* http://assets.pearsonschool.com/asset_mgr/legacy/200931/Problem%20Solving%20Monograph_24324_1.pdf

Carpenter, T., Fennema, E., Franke, M., Levi, L., & Empson, S. (1999). *Children's Mathematics: Cognitively Guided Instruction*. Portsmouth, NH: Heinemann.

Common Core Standards Writing Team (Bill McCullum, lead author). (2012, June 23). *Progressions for the common core state standards in mathematics: Geometry (draft)*. Retrieved from: www.commoncoretools.wordpress.com.

Common Core Standards Writing Team (Bill McCullum, lead author). (2012, June 23). *Progressions for the common core state standards in mathematics: Geometric measurement (draft).* Retrieved from: www.commoncoretools.wordpress.com.

Common Core Standards Writing Team (Bill McCullum, lead author). (2011, June 20). *Progressions for the common core state standards in mathematics: K-3, Categorical data; Grades 2-5, Measurement Data (draft).* Retrieved from: www.commoncoretools.wordpress.com.

Common Core Standards Writing Team (Bill McCullum, lead author). (2011, May 29). *Progressions for the common core state standards in mathematics: K, Counting and cardinality; K-5, operations and algebraic thinking (draft)*. Retrieved from: www.commoncoretools.wordpress.com.

Common Core Standards Writing Team (Bill McCullum, lead author). (2011, April 7). *Progressions for the common core state standards in mathematics: K-5, Number and operations in base ten (draft)*. Retrieved from: www.commoncoretools.wordpress.com.

Common Core Standards Writing Team (Bill McCullum, lead author). (2011, July 12). *Progressions for the common core state standards in mathematics: 3-5 Number and operations - fractions (draft).* Retrieved from: www.commoncoretools.wordpress.com.

Peterson, P. L., Carpenter, T. P., & Loef, M. (1989). *Teachers' Pedagogical Content Beliefs in Mathematics. Cognition and Instruction,* Vol. 6, No. 1, pp. 1-40.

Contact Us!

Dr. Nicki Newton

Email: gigglenook@gmail.com

Website: www.drnicki123.com

Blog: guidedmath.wordpress.com

Made in the USA
San Bernardino, CA
28 October 2013